quick & simple recipes

Soups

Contents

Herbs and Spices for Soup

ALLSPICE The dark allspice berries come whole or ground and have a flavour similar to that of cinnamon, cloves and nutmeg. It works well in a wide variety of soups and stews.

BASIL Best fresh but also available in dried form, basil works well in many dishes but is particularly well suited to tomato-based dishes and sauces, salads and Mediterranean dishes.

BAY LEAVES Are available fresh, dried and ground. They make up part of a bouquet garni and are good when added to meat and poultry dishes, soups, stews, vegetable dishes and stuffing.

BOUQUET GARNI Is a bouquet of fresh parsley, thyme and bay leaves tied with a piece of string or in a small piece of muslin. It is used to flavour casseroles, stews and stocks or sauces.

CAYENNE Is the powdered form of a red chilli pepper said to be native to Cayenne. It is similar in appearance to paprika and can be used sparingly to add a fiery kick to many dishes.

CARDAMOM Has a distinctive sweet rich taste and can be bought whole in the pod, in seed form or ground. This sweet spice is delicious in curries, and can give an aromatic flavour to soups rich in pulses.

CHERVIL Reminiscent of parsley and available either in fresh or dried form, chervil has a faintly sweet spicy flavour and is particularly good in soups, containing beef and chicken, as well as vegetables.

CHILLI Available whole, fresh, dried and in powdered form, red chillies tend to be sweeter in taste than their green counterparts. They are particularly associated with Spanish and Mexican-style cooking and curries.

CHIVES Best used when fresh but also available in dried form, this member of the onion family is ideal for use when a delicate onion flavour is required.

CLOVES Have a very warm sweet pungent aroma and compliment winter soups and stews, rich in root vegetables.

CORIANDER Seeds have an orangey flavour and are available whole or ground. Coriander is particularly delicious with chicken. It can also be used to add extra piquancy to stocks.

CUMIN Available ground or as whole seeds, cumin has a strong, slightly bitter flavour. It compliments many fish, and meat stews.

FENNEL Whole seeds or ground, fennel has a fragrant sweet aniseed flavour and therefore it compliments fish dishes well.

GINGER Comes in many forms but primarily as a fresh root and in dried ground form. The grated fresh root is well suited to Asian and oriental dishes.

LEMON GRASS Available fresh and dried, with a subtle, aromatic, lemony flavour, lemon grass is essential to Thai cooking. It is also delicious when added to soups, poultry and fish dishes.

MARJORAM Often dried, marjoram has a sweet slightly spicy flavour, which tastes fantastic when added to stuffing, meat or tomato-based dishes.

MINT Available fresh or dried, it has a strong sweet aroma which is delicious in dishes containing lamb, white beans or tomato.

MUSTARD SEED These yellow and brown seeds are available whole or ground and are often found in pickles, relishes, cheese dishes, dressings and curries. It works well in stews containing red meat, such as beef.

OREGANO The strongly flavoured dried leaves are similar to marjoram and are used extensively in mediterranean cooking, complementing soups containing beef, mushroom, onion and a variety of vegetables.

PAPRIKA Paprika often comes in two varieties. One is quite sweet and mild and the other has a slight bite to it. Paprika is made from the fruit of the sweet pepper and is good in meat and poultry dishes as well as a garnish.

PARSLEY The stems as well as the leaves of parsley can be used to compliment most savoury dishes as they contain the most flavour. They can also be used as a garnish.

PEPPER This comes in white and black peppercorns and is best freshly ground. Both add flavour to most dishes, sauces and gravies. Black pepper has a more robust flavour, while white pepper has a much more delicate flavour.

ROSEMARY Delicious fresh or dried, the small needle-like leaves have a sweet aroma which is particularly good with lamb and vegetables dishes.

SAFFRON Is traditionally used in paella, rice and cakes but is also delicious with soups containing squashes such as courgette.

SAGE The fresh or dried leaves have a pungent slightly bitter taste which is delicious with pork, poultry, and a variety of beans.

SAVORY This herb resembles thyme, but has a softer flavour that particularly compliments all types of fish and beans.

TARRAGON The fresh or dried leaves of tarragon have a sweet aromatic taste, which is particularly good with poultry, seafood, fish and creamy soups.

THYME Available fresh or dried, thyme has a pungent flavour and is included in bouquet garni. It compliments many meat and poultry dishes as well as dishes such as borscht and clam chowder.

TURMERIC Is obtained from the root of a lily from south-east Asia. This root is ground and has a brilliant yellow colour. It has a bitter peppery flavour and is excellent with bean, chicken, fish or pumpkin soups.

Bacon & Split Pea Soup

Ingredients
Serves 4

50 g/2 oz dried split peas
25 g/1 oz butter
1 garlic clove, peeled and finely chopped
1 medium onion, peeled and thinly sliced
175 g/6 oz long-grain rice
2 tbsp tomato purée
1.1 litres/2 pints vegetable or chicken stock
175 g/6 oz carrots, peeled and finely diced
125 g/4 oz streaky bacon, finely chopped
salt and freshly ground black pepper
2 tbsp freshly chopped parsley
4 tbsp single cream
warm crusty garlic bread, to serve

1 Cover the dried split peas with plenty of cold water, cover loosely and leave to soak for a minimum of 12 hours, preferably overnight.

2 Melt the butter in a heavy-based saucepan, add the garlic and onion and cook for 2–3 minutes, without colouring. Add the rice, drained split peas and tomato purée and cook for 2–3 minutes, stirring constantly to prevent sticking. Add the stock, bring to the boil, then reduce the heat and simmer for 20–25 minutes, or until the rice and peas are tender. Remove from the heat and leave to cool.

3 Blend about three-quarters of the soup in a food processor or blender to form a smooth purée. Pour the purée into the remaining soup in the saucepan. Add the carrots to the saucepan and cook for a further 10–12 minutes, or until the carrots are tender.

4 Meanwhile, place the bacon in a non-stick frying pan and cook over a gentle heat until the bacon is crisp. Remove and drain on absorbent kitchen paper.

5 Season the soup with salt and pepper to taste, then stir in the parsley and cream. Reheat for 2–3 minutes, then ladle into soup bowls. Sprinkle with the bacon and serve immediately with warm garlic bread.

Carrot & Ginger Soup

Ingredients
Serves 4

4 slices of bread, crusts removed
1 tsp yeast extract
2 tsp olive oil
1 onion, peeled and chopped
1 garlic clove, peeled and crushed
½ tsp ground ginger
450 g/1 lb carrots, peeled and chopped
1 litre/1¾ pint vegetable stock
2.5 cm/1 inch piece of root ginger, peeled and finely grated
salt and freshly ground black pepper
1 tbsp lemon juice

To garnish

chives
lemon zest

CHEF'S TIP
Serve with a spoonful of lightly whipped or sour cream, for a special occasion.

1 Preheat the oven to 180°C/ 350°F/Gas Mark 4. Roughly chop the bread. Dissolve the yeast extract in 2 tablespoons of warm water and mix with the bread.

2 Spread the bread cubes over a lightly oiled baking tray and bake for 20 minutes, turning half way through. Remove from the oven and reserve.

3 Heat the oil in a large saucepan. Gently cook the onion and garlic for 3–4 minutes.

4 Stir in the ground ginger and cook for 1 minute to release the flavour.

5 Add the chopped carrots, then stir in the stock and the fresh ginger. Simmer gently for 15 minutes.

6 Remove from the heat and allow to cool a little. Blend until smooth, then season to taste with salt and pepper. Stir in the lemon juice. Garnish with the chives and lemon zest and serve immediately.

Cawl

Ingredients
Serves 4–6

700 g/1½ lb scrag end of lamb or best end of neck chops
pinch of salt
2 large onions, peeled and thinly sliced
3 large potatoes, peeled and cut into chunks
2 parsnips, peeled and cut into chunks
1 swede, peeled and cut into chunks
3 large carrots, peeled and cut into chunks
2 leeks, trimmed and sliced
freshly ground black pepper
4 tbsp freshly chopped parsley
warm crusty bread, to serve

1 Put the lamb in a large saucepan, cover with cold water and bring to the boil. Add a generous pinch of salt. Simmer gently for 1½ hours, then set aside to cool completely, preferably overnight.

2 The next day, skim the fat off the surface of the lamb liquid and discard. Return the saucepan to the heat and bring back to the boil. Simmer for 5 minutes. Add the onions, potatoes, parsnips, swede and carrots and return to the boil. Reduce the heat, cover and cook for about 20 minutes, stirring occasionally.

3 Add the leeks and season to taste with salt and pepper. Cook for a further 10 minutes, or until all the vegetables are tender.

4 Using a slotted spoon, remove the meat from the saucepan and take the meat off the bone. Discard the bones and any gristle, then return the meat to the pan. Adjust the seasoning to taste, stir in the parsley, then serve immediately with plenty of warm crusty bread.

CHEF'S TIP
Welsh mountain lamb is best for this dish, as the meat is infused with the flavour of the wild rosemary and thyme that the sheep graze on.

Classic Minestrone

Ingredients
Serves 6–8

25 g/1 oz butter
3 tbsp olive oil
3 rashers streaky bacon
1 large onion, peeled
1 garlic clove, peeled
1 celery stick, trimmed
2 carrots, peeled
400 g can chopped
    tomatoes
1.1 litre/2 pints chicken
    stock
175 g/6 oz green
    cabbage, finely
    shredded
50 g/2 oz French beans,
    trimmed and halved
3 tbsp frozen petits
    pois
50 g/2 oz spaghetti,
    broken into short
    pieces
salt and freshly ground
    black pepper
Parmesan cheese
    shavings, to garnish
crusty bread, to serve

CHEF'S TIP
For a vegetarian version,
omit the bacon and use
vegetable stock and a
vegetarian cheese.

1 Heat the butter and olive oil together in a large saucepan. Chop the bacon and add to the saucepan. Cook for 3–4 minutes, then remove with a slotted spoon and reserve.

2 Finely chop the onion, garlic, celery and carrots and add to the saucepan, one ingredient at a time, stirring well after each addition. Cover and cook gently for 8–10 minutes, until the vegetables are softened.

3 Add the chopped tomatoes, with their juice and the stock, bring to the boil then cover the saucepan with a lid, reduce the heat and simmer gently for about 20 minutes.

4 Stir in the cabbage, beans, peas and spaghetti pieces. Cover and simmer for a further 20 minutes, or until all the ingredients are tender. Season to taste with salt and pepper.

5 Return the cooked bacon to the saucepan and bring the soup to the boil. Serve the soup immediately with Parmesan cheese shavings sprinkled on the top and plenty of crusty bread to accompany it.

Clear Chicken & Mushroom Soup

Ingredients
Serves 4

2 large chicken legs,
  about 450 g/1 lb total
  weight
1 tbsp groundnut oil
1 tsp sesame oil
1 onion, peeled and very
  thinly sliced
2.5 cm/1 inch piece root
  ginger, peeled and
  very finely chopped
1.1 litres/2 pints clear
  chicken stock
1 lemon grass stalk,
  bruised
50 g/2 oz long-grain
  rice
75 g/3 oz button
  mushrooms, wiped
  and finely sliced
4 spring onions,
  trimmed, cut into
  5 cm/2 inch pieces
  and shredded
1 tbsp dark soy sauce
4 tbsp dry sherry
salt and freshly ground
  black pepper

CHEF'S TIP
Miso makes a tasty and
nutritious alternative to
chicken stock.

1 Skin the chicken legs and remove any fat. Cut each in half to make 2 thigh and 2 drumstick portions and reserve. Heat the groundnut and sesame oils in a large saucepan. Add the sliced onion and cook gently for 10 minutes, or until soft but not beginning to colour.

2 Add the chopped ginger to the saucepan and cook for about 30 seconds, stirring all the time to prevent it sticking, then pour in the stock. Add the chicken pieces and the lemon grass, cover and simmer gently for 15 minutes. Stir in the rice and cook for a further 15 minutes or until the chicken is cooked.

3 Remove the chicken from the saucepan and leave until cool enough to handle. Finely shred the flesh, then return to the saucepan with the mushrooms, spring onions, soy sauce and sherry. Simmer for 5 minutes, or until the rice and mushrooms are tender. Remove the lemon grass.

4 Season the soup to taste with salt and pepper. Ladle into warmed serving bowls, making sure each has an equal amount of shredded chicken and vegetables and serve immediately.

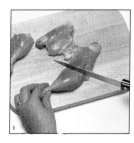

Cream of Pumpkin Soup

Ingredients
Serves 4

900 g/2 lb pumpkin flesh (after peeling and discarding the seeds)
4 tbsp olive oil
1 large onion, peeled
1 leek, trimmed
1 carrot, peeled
2 celery sticks
4 garlic cloves, peeled and crushed
1.7 litres/3 pints water
salt and freshly ground black pepper
¼ tsp freshly grated nutmeg
150 ml/¼ pint single cream
¼ tsp cayenne pepper
warm herby bread, to serve

CHEF'S TIP
If pumpkin is unavailable you can use Butternut squash instead.

1 Cut the skinned and de-seeded pumpkin flesh into 2.5 cm/1 inch cubes. Heat the olive oil in a large saucepan and cook the pumpkin for 2–3 minutes, coating it completely with oil. Chop the onion and leek finely and cut the carrot and celery into small dice.

2 Add the vegetables to the saucepan with the garlic and cook, stirring for 5 minutes, or until they have begun to soften. Cover the vegetables with the water and bring to the boil. Season with plenty of salt and pepper and the nutmeg, cover and simmer for 15–20 minutes, or until all of the vegetables are tender.

3 When the vegetables are tender, remove from the heat, cool slightly then pour into a food processor or blender. Liquidise to form a smooth purée then pass through a sieve into a clean saucepan.

4 Adjust the seasoning to taste and add all but 2 tablespoons of the cream and enough water to obtain the correct consistency. Bring the soup to boiling point, add the cayenne pepper and serve immediately swirled with cream and warm herby bread.

Cream of Spinach Soup

Ingredients
Serves 6–8

1 large onion, peeled and chopped

5 large plump garlic cloves, peeled and chopped

2 medium potatoes, peeled and chopped

750 ml/1¼ pints cold water

1 tsp salt

450 g/1 lb spinach, washed and large stems removed

50 g/2 oz butter

3 tbsp flour

750 ml/1¼ pints milk

½ tsp freshly grated nutmeg

freshly ground black pepper

6–8 tbsp crème fraîche or soured cream

warm foccacia bread, to serve

1 Place the onion, garlic and potatoes in a large saucepan and cover with the cold water. Add half the salt and bring to the boil. Cover and simmer for 15–20 minutes, or until the potatoes are tender. Remove from the heat and add the spinach. Cover and set aside for 10 minutes.

2 Slowly melt the butter in another saucepan, add the flour and cook over a low heat for about 2 minutes. Remove the saucepan from the heat and add the milk, a little at a time, stirring continuously. Return to the heat and cook, stirring continuously, for 5–8 minutes, or until the sauce is smooth and slightly thickened. Add the freshly grated nutmeg, or to taste.

3 Blend the cooled potato and spinach mixture in a food processor or blender to a smooth purée, then return to the saucepan and gradually stir in the white sauce. Season to taste with salt and pepper and gently reheat, taking care not to allow the soup to boil. Ladle into soup bowls and top with spoonfuls of crème fraîche or soured cream. Serve immediately with warm foccacia bread.

CHEF'S TIP
For the best results always look for spinach with fresh, crisp, dark-green leaves and use within 2 days of purchase.

Creamy Caribbean Chicken & Coconut Soup

Ingredients
Serves 4

6–8 spring onions
2 garlic cloves
1 red chilli
175 g/6 oz cooked
    chicken, shredded
    or diced
2 tbsp vegetable oil
1 tsp ground turmeric
300 ml/½ pint coconut
    milk
900 ml/1½ pints
    chicken stock
50 g/2 oz small soup
    pasta or spaghetti,
    broken into small
    pieces
½ lemon, sliced
salt and freshly ground
    black pepper
1–2 tbsp freshly
    chopped coriander
sprigs of fresh
    coriander, to garnish

1 Trim the spring onions and thinly slice; peel the garlic and finely chop. Cut off the top from the chilli, slit down the side and remove seeds and membrane, then finely chop and reserve.

2 Remove and discard any skin or bones from the cooked chicken and shred using two forks and reserve.

3 Heat a large wok, add the oil and when hot add the spring onions, garlic and chilli and stir-fry for 2 minutes, or until the onion has softened. Stir in the turmeric and cook for 1 minute.

4 Blend the coconut milk with the chicken stock until smooth, then pour into the wok. Add the pasta or spaghetti with the lemon slices and bring to the boil.

5 Simmer, half-covered, for 10–12 minutes, or until the pasta is tender; stir occasionally.

6 Remove the lemon slices from the wok and add the chicken. Season to taste with salt and pepper and simmer for 2–3 minutes, or until the chicken is heated through thoroughly.

7 Stir in the chopped coriander and ladle into heated bowls. Garnish with sprigs of fresh coriander and serve immediately.

Creamy Chicken & Tofu Soup

Ingredients
Serves 4–6

225 g/8 oz firm tofu, drained

3 tbsp groundnut oil

1 garlic clove, peeled and crushed

2.5 cm/1 inch piece root ginger, peeled and finely chopped

2.5 cm/1 inch piece fresh galangal, peeled and finely sliced (if available)

1 lemon grass stalk, bruised

¼ tsp ground turmeric

600 ml/1 pint chicken stock

600 ml/1 pint coconut milk

225 g/8 oz cauliflower, cut into tiny florets

1 medium carrot, peeled and cut into thin matchsticks

125 g/4 oz green beans, trimmed and cut in half

75 g/3 oz thin egg noodles

225 g/8 oz cooked chicken, shredded

salt and freshly ground black pepper

1 Cut the tofu into 1 cm/½ inch cubes, then pat dry on absorbent kitchen paper.

2 Heat 1 tablespoon of the oil in a nonstick frying pan. Fry the tofu in 2 batches for 3–4 minutes or until golden brown. Remove, drain on absorbent kitchen paper and reserve.

3 Heat the remaining oil in a large saucepan. Add the garlic, ginger, galangal and lemon grass and cook for about 30 seconds. Stir in the turmeric, then pour in the stock and coconut milk and bring to the boil. Reduce the heat to a gentle simmer, add the cauliflower and carrots and simmer for 10 minutes. Add the green beans and simmer for a further 5 minutes.

4 Meanwhile, bring a large saucepan of lightly salted water to the boil. Add the noodles, turn off the heat, cover and leave to cook, or cook according to the packet instructions.

5 Remove the lemon grass from the soup. Drain the noodles and stir into the soup with the chicken and browned tofu. Season to taste with salt and pepper, then simmer gently for 2–3 minutes or until heated through. Serve immediately in warmed soup bowls.

Curried Parsnip Soup

Ingredients
Serves 4

1 tsp cumin seeds
2 tsp coriander seeds
1 tsp oil
1 onion, peeled and
   chopped
1 garlic clove, peeled
   and crushed
½ tsp turmeric
¼ tsp chilli powder
1 cinnamon stick
450 g/1 lb parsnips,
   peeled and chopped
1 litre/1¾ pint
   vegetable stock
salt and freshly ground
   black pepper
2–3 tbsp low-fat
   natural yogurt,
   to serve
fresh coriander leaves,
   to garnish

1 In a small frying pan, dry-fry the cumin and coriander seeds over a moderately high heat for 1–2 minutes. Shake the pan during cooking until the seeds are lightly toasted.

2 Reserve until cooled. Grind the toasted seeds in a pestle and mortar.

3 Heat the oil in a saucepan. Cook the onion until softened and starting to turn golden.

4 Add the garlic, turmeric, chilli powder and cinnamon stick to the pan. Continue to cook for a further minute.

5 Add the parsnips and stir well. Pour in the stock and bring to the boil. Cover and simmer for 15 minutes or until the parsnips are cooked.

6 Allow the soup to cool. Once cooled, remove the cinnamon stick and discard.

7 Blend the soup in a food processor until very smooth.

8 Transfer to a saucepan and reheat gently. Season to taste with salt and pepper. Garnish with fresh coriander and serve immediately with the yogurt.

Hot & Sour Mushroom Soup

Ingredients
Serves 4

4 tbsp sunflower oil
3 garlic cloves, peeled
   and finely chopped
3 shallots, peeled and
   finely chopped
2 large red chillies,
   deseeded and finely
   chopped
1 tbsp soft brown sugar
large pinch of salt
1 litre/1¾ pints
   vegetable stock
250 g/9 oz Thai
   fragrant rice
5 kaffir lime leaves, torn
2 tbsp soy sauce
grated rind and juice of
   1 lemon
250 g/9 oz oyster
   mushrooms, wiped
   and cut into pieces
2 tbsp freshly chopped
   coriander

To garnish

2 green chillies,
   deseeded and finely
   chopped
3 spring onions,
   trimmed and finely
   chopped

1 Heat the oil in a frying pan, add the garlic and shallots and cook until golden brown and starting to crisp. Remove from the pan and reserve. Add the chillies to the pan and cook until they start to change colour.

2 Place the garlic, shallots and chillies in a food processor or blender and blend to a smooth purée with 150 ml /¼ pint water. Pour the purée back into the pan, add the sugar with a large pinch of salt, then cook gently, stirring, until dark in colour. Take care not to burn the mixture.

3 Pour the stock into a large saucepan, add the garlic purée, rice, lime leaves, soy sauce and the lemon rind and juice. Bring to the boil, then reduce the heat, cover and simmer gently for about 10 minutes.

4 Add the mushrooms and simmer for a further 10 minutes, or until the mushrooms and rice are tender. Remove the lime leaves, stir in the chopped coriander and ladle into bowls. Place the chopped green chillies and spring onions in small bowls and serve separately to sprinkle on top of the soup.

Italian Bean Soup

Ingredients
Serves 4

2 tsp olive oil
1 leek, washed and chopped
1 garlic clove, peeled and crushed
2 tsp dried oregano
75 g/3 oz green beans, trimmed and cut into bite-size pieces
410 g can cannellini beans, drained and rinsed
75 g/3 oz small pasta shapes
1 litre/1¾ pint vegetable stock
8 cherry tomatoes
salt and freshly ground black pepper
3 tbsp freshly shredded basil

1 Heat the oil in a large saucepan. Add the leek, garlic and oregano and cook gently for 5 minutes, stirring occasionally.

2 Stir in the green beans and the cannellini beans. Sprinkle in the pasta and pour in the stock.

3 Bring the stock mixture to the boil, then reduce the heat to a simmer.

4 Cook for 12–15 minutes or until the vegetables are tender and the pasta is cooked to al dente. Stir occasionally.

5 In a heavy-based frying pan, dry-fry the tomatoes over a high heat until they soften and the skins begin to blacken.

6 Gently crush the tomatoes in the pan with the back of a spoon and add to the soup.

7 Season to taste with salt and pepper. Stir in the shredded basil and serve immediately.

CHEF'S TIP
If you need to replace fresh herbs with the dried variety, remember that one teaspoon of dried herbs is equivalent to one tablespoon of fresh herbs.

Mushroom & Sherry Soup

Ingredients
Serves 4

4 slices day old white bread
zest of ½ lemon
1 tbsp lemon juice
salt and freshly ground black pepper
125 g/4 oz assorted wild mushrooms, lightly rinsed
125 g/4 oz baby button mushrooms, wiped
2 tsp olive oil
1 garlic clove, peeled and crushed
6 spring onions, trimmed and diagonally sliced
600 ml/1 pint chicken stock
4 tbsp dry sherry
1 tbsp freshly snipped chives, to garnish

1 Preheat the oven to 180°C/ 350°F/Gas Mark 4. Remove the crusts from the bread and cut the bread into small cubes.

2 In a large bowl toss the cubes of bread with the lemon rind and juice, 2 tablespoons of water and plenty of freshly ground black pepper.

3 Spread the bread cubes on to a lightly oiled, large baking tray and bake for 20 minutes until golden and crisp.

4 If the wild mushrooms are small, leave some whole. Otherwise, thinly slice all the mushrooms and reserve.

5 Heat the oil in a saucepan. Add the garlic and spring onions and cook for 1–2 minutes.

6 Add the mushrooms and cook for 3–4 minutes until they start to soften. Add the chicken stock and stir to mix.

7 Bring to the boil, then reduce the heat to a gentle simmer. Cover and cook for 10 minutes.

8 Stir in the sherry, and season to taste with a little salt and pepper. Pour into warmed bowls, sprinkle over the chives, and serve immediately with the lemon croûtons.

Potatoes, Leek & Rosemary Soup

Ingredients
Serves 4

50 g/2 oz butter

450 g/1 lb leeks, trimmed and finely sliced

700 g/1½ lb potatoes, peeled and roughly chopped

900 ml/1½ pints vegetable stock

4 sprigs of fresh rosemary

450 ml/¾ pint full-cream milk

2 tbsp freshly chopped parsley

2 tbsp crème fraîche

salt and freshly ground black pepper

wholemeal rolls, to serve

1 Melt the butter in a large saucepan, add the leeks and cook gently for 5 minutes, stirring frequently. Remove 1 tablespoon of the cooked leeks and reserve for garnishing.

2 Add the potatoes, vegetable stock, rosemary sprigs and milk. Bring to the boil, then reduce the heat, cover and simmer gently for 20–25 minutes, or until the vegetables are tender.

3 Cool for 10 minutes. Discard the rosemary, then pour into a food processor or blender and blend well to form a smooth-textured soup.

4 Return the soup to the cleaned saucepan and stir in the chopped parsley and crème fraîche. Season to taste with salt and pepper. If the soup is too thick, stir in a little more milk or water. Reheat gently without boiling, then ladle into warm soup bowls. Garnish the soup with the reserved leeks and serve immediately with wholemeal rolls.

CHEF'S TIP
This soup is delicious served either hot or cold. To serve cold, chill for at least two hours in the refrigerator.

Pumpkin & Smoked Haddock Soup

Ingredients

Serves 4–6

2 tbsp olive oil

1 medium onion, peeled and chopped

2 garlic cloves, peeled and chopped

3 celery stalks, trimmed and chopped

700 g/1½ lb pumpkin, peeled, deseeded and cut into chunks

450 g/1 lb potatoes, peeled and cut into chunks

750 ml/1¼ pints chicken stock, heated

125 ml/4 fl oz dry sherry

200 g/7 oz smoked haddock fillet

150 ml/¼ pint milk

freshly ground black pepper

2 tbsp freshly chopped parsley

1 Heat the oil in a large heavy-based saucepan and gently cook the onion, garlic, and celery for about 10 minutes. This will release the sweetness but not colour the vegetables. Add the pumpkin and potatoes to the saucepan and stir to coat the vegetables with the oil.

2 Gradually pour in the stock and bring to the boil. Cover, then reduce the heat and simmer for 25 minutes, stirring occasionally. Stir in the dry sherry, then remove the saucepan from the heat and leave to cool for 5–10 minutes.

3 Blend the mixture in a food processor or blender to form a chunky purée and return to the cleaned saucepan.

4 Meanwhile, place the fish in a shallow frying pan. Pour in the milk with 3 tablespoons of water and bring to almost boiling point. Reduce the heat, cover and simmer for 6 minutes, or until the fish is cooked and flakes easily. Remove from the heat and, using a slotted spoon remove the fish from the liquid, reserving both liquid and fish.

5 Discard the skin and any bones from the fish and flake into pieces. Stir the fish liquid into the soup, together with the flaked fish. Season with freshly ground black pepper, stir in the parsley and serve immediately.

Rich Tomato Soup with Roasted Red Peppers

Ingredients
Serves 4

2 tsp light olive oil

700 g/1½ lb red peppers, halved and deseeded

450 g/1 lb ripe plum tomatoes, halved

2 onions, unpeeled and quartered

4 garlic cloves, unpeeled

600 ml/1 pint chicken stock

salt and freshly ground black pepper

4 tbsp soured cream

1 tbsp freshly shredded basil

1 Preheat oven to 200°C/ 400°F/Gas Mark 6. Lightly oil a roasting tin with 1 teaspoon of the olive oil. Place the peppers and tomatoes cut side down in the roasting tin with the onion quarters and the garlic cloves. Spoon over the remaining oil.

2 Bake in the preheated oven for 30 minutes, or until the skins on the peppers have started to blacken and blister. Allow the vegetables to cool for about 10 minutes, then remove the skins, stalks and seeds from the peppers. Peel away the skins from the tomatoes and onions and squeeze out the garlic.

3 Place the cooked vegetables into a blender or food processor and blend until smooth. Add the stock and blend again to form a smooth purée. Pour the puréed soup through a sieve, if a smooth soup is preferred, then pour into a saucepan. Bring to the boil, simmer gently for 2–3 minutes, and season to taste with salt and pepper. Serve hot with a swirl of soured cream and a sprinkling of shredded basil on the top.

CHEF'S TIP
To remove the pepper skins more easily, put them into a plastic bag, on removal from the oven, and leave to cool.

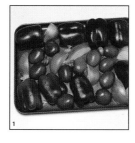

Rocket & Potato Soup with Garlic Croûtons

Ingredients
Serves 4

700 g/1½ lb baby new potatoes
1.1 litres/2 pints chicken or vegetable stock
50 g/2 oz rocket leaves
125 g/4 oz thick white sliced bread
50 g/2 oz unsalted butter
1 tsp groundnut oil
2–4 garlic cloves, peeled and chopped
125 g/4 oz stale ciabatta bread, with the crusts removed
4 tbsp olive oil
salt and freshly ground black pepper
2 tbsp Parmesan cheese, finely grated

CHEF'S TIP
If rocket is unavailable use watercress or baby spinach instead.

1 Place the potatoes in a large saucepan, cover with the stock and simmer gently for 10 minutes. Add the rocket leaves and simmer for a further 5–10 minutes, or until the potatoes are soft and the rocket has wilted.

2 Meanwhile, make the croûtons. Cut the thick, white sliced bread into small cubes and reserve. Heat the butter and groundnut oil in a small frying pan and cook the garlic for 1 minute, stirring well. Remove the garlic. Add the bread cubes to the butter and oil mixture in the frying pan and sauté, stirring continuously, until they are golden brown. Drain the croûtons on absorbent kitchen paper and reserve.

3 Cut the ciabatta bread into small dice and stir into the soup. Cover the saucepan and leave to stand for 10 minutes, or until the bread has absorbed a lot of the liquid.

4 Stir in the olive oil, season to taste with salt and pepper and serve at once with a few of the garlic croûtons scattered over the top and a little grated Parmesan cheese.

Swede, Turnip, Parsnip & Potato Soup

Ingredients
Serves 4

2 large onions, peeled
25 g/1 oz butter
2 medium carrots,
    peeled and roughly
    chopped
175 g/6 oz swede,
    peeled and roughly
    chopped
125 g/4 oz turnip, peeled
    and roughly chopped
125 g/4 oz parsnips,
    peeled and roughly
    chopped
175 g/6 oz potatoes,
    peeled
1 litre/1¾ pints
    vegetable stock
½ tsp freshly grated
    nutmeg
salt and freshly ground
    black pepper
4 tbsp vegetable oil,
    for frying
125 ml/4 fl oz double
    cream
warm crusty bread,
    to serve

CHEF'S TIP
For a lower-fat version of
this soup use semi-
skimmed milk instead of
cream, when reheating.

1 Finely chop 1 onion. Melt the butter in a large saucepan and add the onion, carrots, swede, turnip, parsnip and potatoes. Cover and cook gently for about 10 minutes, without colouring. Stir occasionally during this time.

2 Add the stock and season to taste with the nutmeg, salt and pepper. Cover and bring to the boil, then reduce the heat and simmer gently for 15–20 minutes, or until the vegetables are tender. Remove from the heat and leave to cool for 30 minutes.

3 Heat the oil in a large heavy-based frying pan. Add the onions and cook over a medium heat, for about 2–3 minutes, stirring frequently, until golden brown. Remove the onions with a slotted spoon and drain well on absorbent kitchen paper. As they cool, they will turn crispy.

4 Pour the cooled soup into a food processor or blender and process to form a smooth purée. Return to the cleaned pan, adjust the seasoning, then stir in the cream. Gently reheat and top with the crispy onions. Serve immediately with chunks of bread.

Sweetcorn & Crab Soup

Ingredients
Serves 4

450 g/1 lb fresh corn-on-the-cob
1.3 litres/2¼ pints chicken stock
2–3 spring onions, trimmed and finely chopped
1 cm/½ inch piece fresh root ginger, peeled and finely chopped
1 tbsp dry sherry or Chinese rice wine
2–3 tsp soy sauce
1 tsp soft light brown sugar
salt and freshly ground black pepper
2 tsp cornflour
225 g/8 oz white crabmeat, fresh or canned
1 medium egg white
1 tsp sesame oil
1–2 tbsp freshly chopped coriander

1 Wash the corns cobs and dry. Using a sharp knife and holding the corn cobs at an angle to the cutting board, cut down along the cobs to remove the kernels, then scrape the cobs to remove any excess milky residue. Put the kernels and the milky residue into a large wok.

2 Add the chicken stock to the wok and place over a high heat. Bring to the boil, stirring and pressing some of the kernels against the side of the wok to squeeze out the starch to help thicken the soup. Simmer for 15 minutes, stirring occasionally.

3 Add the spring onions, ginger, sherry or Chinese rice wine, soy sauce and brown sugar to the wok and season to taste with salt and pepper. Simmer for a further 5 minutes, stirring occasionally.

4 Blend the cornflour with 1 tablespoon of cold water to form a smooth paste and whisk into the soup. Return to the boil, then simmer over a medium heat until thickened.

5 Add the crabmeat, stirring until blended. Beat the egg white with the sesame oil and stir into the soup in a slow steady stream, stirring constantly. Stir in the chopped coriander and serve immediately.

Thai Hot & Sour Prawn Soup

Ingredients
Serves 6

700 g/1½ lb large raw
    prawns
2 tbsp vegetable oil
3–4 stalks lemon grass,
    outer leaves
    discarded and
    coarsely chopped
2.5 cm/1 inch piece
    fresh root ginger,
    peeled and finely
    chopped
2–3 garlic cloves, peeled
    and crushed
small bunch fresh
    coriander, leaves
    stripped and
    reserved, stems finely
    chopped
½ tsp freshly ground
    black pepper
1.8 litres/3¼ pints water
1–2 small red chillies,
    deseeded and thinly
    sliced
1–2 small green chillies,
    deseeded and thinly
    sliced
6 kaffir lime leaves,
    thinly shredded
4 spring onions,
    trimmed and
    diagonally sliced
1–2 tbsp Thai fish sauce
1–2 tbsp freshly
    squeezed lime juice

1 Remove the heads from the prawns by twisting away from the
body and reserve. Peel the prawns, leaving the tails on and reserve
the shells with the heads. Using a sharp knife, remove the black
vein from the back of the prawns. Rinse and dry the prawns and
reserve. Rinse and dry the heads and shells.

2 Heat a wok, add the oil and, when hot, add the prawn heads and
shells, the lemon grass, ginger, garlic, coriander stems and black
pepper and stir-fry for 2–3 minutes, or until the prawn heads and
shells turn pink and all the ingredients are coloured.

3 Carefully add the water to the wok and return to the boil,
skimming off any scum which rises to the surface. Simmer over
a medium heat for 10 minutes or until slightly reduced. Strain
through a fine sieve and return the clear prawn stock to the wok.

4 Bring the stock back to the boil and add the reserved prawns,
chillies, lime leaves and spring onions and simmer for 3 minutes, or
until the prawns turn pink. Season with the fish sauce and lime
juice. Spoon into heated soup bowls, dividing the prawns evenly
and float a few coriander leaves over the surface.

Tomato & Basil Soup

Ingredients
Serves 4

1.1 kg/ 2½ lb ripe tomatoes, cut in half
2 garlic cloves
1 tsp olive oil
1 tbsp balsamic vinegar
1 tbsp dark brown sugar
1 tbsp tomato purée
300 ml/½ pint vegetable stock
6 tbsp low-fat natural yogurt
2 tbsp freshly chopped basil
salt and freshly ground black pepper
small basil leaves, to garnish

1 Preheat the oven to 200°C/ 400°F/Gas Mark 6. Evenly spread the tomatoes and unpeeled garlic in a single layer in a large roasting tin.

2 Mix the oil and vinegar together. Drizzle over the tomatoes and sprinkle with the dark brown sugar.

3 Roast the tomatoes in the preheated oven for 20 minutes until tender and lightly charred in places.

4 Remove from the oven and allow to cool slightly. When cool enough to handle, squeeze the softened flesh of the garlic from the papery skin. Place with the charred tomatoes in a nylon sieve over a saucepan.

5 Press the garlic and tomato through the sieve with the back of a wooden spoon.

6 When all the flesh has been sieved, add the tomato purée and vegetable stock to the pan. Heat gently, stirring occasionally.

7 In a small bowl beat the yogurt and basil together and season to taste with salt and pepper. Stir the basil yogurt into the soup. Garnish with basil leaves and serve immediately.

CHEF'S TIP
For the most intense flavour, use the sweetest type of tomatoes available.

White Bean Soup with Parmesan Croûtons

Ingredients
Serves 4

3 thick slices of white bread, cut into 1 cm/½ inch cubes

3 tbsp groundnut oil

2 tbsp Parmesan cheese, finely grated

1 tbsp light olive oil

1 large onion, peeled and finely chopped

50 g/2 oz unsmoked bacon lardons (or thick slices of bacon, diced)

1 tbsp fresh thyme leaves

2 x 400 g cannellini beans, drained

900 ml/1½ pints chicken stock

salt and freshly ground black pepper

1 tbsp prepared pesto sauce

50 g/2 oz piece of pepperoni sausage, diced

1 tbsp fresh lemon juice

1 tbsp fresh basil, roughly shredded

1 Preheat oven to 200°C/ 400°F/Gas Mark 6. Place the cubes of bread in a bowl and pour over the groundnut oil. Stir to coat the bread, then sprinkle over the Parmesan cheese. Place on a lightly oiled baking tray and bake in the preheated oven for 10 minutes, or until crisp and golden.

2 Heat the olive oil in a large saucepan and cook the onion for 4–5 minutes until softened. Add the bacon and thyme and cook for a further 3 minutes. Stir in the beans, stock and black pepper and simmer gently for 5 minutes.

3 Place half the bean mixture and liquid into a food processor and blend until smooth.

4 Return the purée to the saucepan. Stir in the pesto sauce, pepperoni sausage and lemon juice and season to taste with salt and pepper.

5 Return the soup to the heat and cook for a further 2–3 minutes, or until piping hot. Place some of the beans in each serving bowl and add a ladleful of soup. Garnish with shredded basil and serve immediately with the croûtons scattered over the top.

This is a **STAR FIRE** book
This edition published in 2010

10 12 14 13 11

1 3 5 7 9 10 8 6 4 2

Star Fire is part of The Foundry Creative Media Company Limited
Crabtree Hall, Crabtree Lane, Fulham, London, SW6 6TY
Visit the Foundry website: *www.foundry.co.uk*

Copyright © The Foundry 2010

ISBN: 978-1-84786-797-1

The CIP record for this book is available from the British Library

Printed in China

ACKNOWLEDGEMENTS

Authors: Catherine Atkinson, Juliet Barker, Liz Martin,
Gina Steer, Carol Tennant, Mari Mereid Williams,
Elizabeth Wolf-Cohen, Simone Wright

Editorial Consultant: Gina Steer

Editors: Michelle Clare, Karen Fitzpatrick, Vicky Garrard, Julia Rolf
Photography: Colin Bowling and Paul Forrester

Home Economists and Stylists: Jacqueline Bellefontaine,
Mandy Phipps, Vicki Smallwood and Penny Stephens

Design Team: Helen Courtney, Jennifer Bishop,
Lucy Bradbury and Chris Herbert

All props supplied by Barbara Stewart at Surfaces

NOTE

Recipes using uncooked eggs should be avoided by infants, the
elderly, pregnant women and anyone suffering from an illness.